Strattomics
A Practical Guide to Strategies and Tactics for our Agile World

Huw Morris

Copyright © 2014 Huw Morris

All rights reserved.

ISBN: 1495243818
ISBN-13: 978-1495243813

DEDICATION

To the individuals who are committed to developing the efficiency, effectiveness and engagement of the people in their enterprise.

CONTENTS

	Acknowledgments	i
1	Introduction	1
2	Continuous Improvement	3
3	Raising Agility	27
4	Building Stakeholder Commitment	59
5	Conclusions	71
6	Bibliography	73

ACKNOWLEDGMENTS

As I wrote this book I reflected on the people who have helped me learn and given me opportunities to improve a broad spectrum of enterprises - throughout my development. Starting with school in Hertfordshire and college in Kent, during my Royal Air Force career in the UK, Germany and the USA, while at Business School at Henley, business school teaching in Somerset and then while working with Andersen Consulting / Accenture, the Financial Reporting Council, LECG and FTI Consulting and most recently as I launched Efficienarta. Thank you all.

1 INTRODUCTION

"The competitive heat has been turned up by new technology. But cool heads are still needed when dealing with disrupters."

The Economist 11 January 2014

Enterprises of all types and all sizes are facing an increasingly challenging competitive environment - not least due to the impact of technology and evolving social norms. The hypothesis behind this book is that flourishing enterprises excel at their current activities, spot changes in their markets early and develop their agility to embrace the new threats and opportunities. These necessitate ever more effective engagement with employees and the full spectrum of your stakeholders. Competitive advantage or new business streams can flow from ideas from anywhere within enterprises, but only if the culture encourages people to spot opportunity and if the managers recognise them.

I like to relate the development of businesses to expeditions through mountain ranges. The better we are at the basics, the quicker we can climb each mountain without accidents. The fitter we are, the more alert we are to changes in our environment, as we have the capacity to "take in" more and not just concentrate on putting one foot in front of the other. The more agile we are, the better we can respond to new peaks as they emerge.

This book includes a selection of practical tools and techniques that I have used and that I believe will help business leaders to retain (in the words of the Economist) "cool heads" as they climb the mountains of competition. It is targeted primarily at individuals who have not been to business school and endeavours to help leaders enlarge their personal toolbox of business leadership techniques and not least to "ask the right questions". It has three central themes:

- Continuous Improvement of existing products and services,
- Raising agility to promote proactive evolution of the business by spotting and embracing changes in your competitive environment (Enterprise Effectiveness),
- Positively building stakeholder engagement – amongst employees, executives, non-executive directors, shareholders, and local communities etc.

Throughout the book tools, methods and approaches are introduced that, if engrained into your enterprise DNA, strategies, tactics and working practices:

- help raise the quality of existing products and services,
- grow agility to help you compete better in our agile world and
- enhance relationships with your full spectrum of stakeholders.

The presentation of these techniques builds on Executive workshops that I have delivered over the last two years and the experience I gained over 30 years in management roles in private and public sector organisations. At the end of each chapter there is a link to our website that contains electronic templates and job aids relevant to the chapter and some suggestions for further reading.

For people who either use or are considering using management consultants this book can help you be a more effective buyer - not least by helping you scope the particular areas where external assistance can add more value than cost.

2 CONTINUOUS IMPROVEMENT

> *"Process Improvement is aligned around what our customers value, which translates into business objectives that flow from the enterprise through the organization level down to individuals. …. We monitor a handful of key process metrics to ensure that we are making progress toward achieving corporate objectives. …. the ability to embrace change is not only core to continuous improvement but is indeed a foundation for competitive advantage."*
>
> *GE Capital*

Most enterprises face intensely competitive environments where customer expectations are growing more demanding. Enterprises that have "continuous improvement" in the DNA - as opposed to the "we have always done it this way" mentality - have a foundation for both "raising the bar" in meeting client expectations and reducing the cost of quality. In this chapter I will introduce a number of techniques that I believe are useful additions to the "tool boxes" of those responsible for delivering products and services of all kinds. Using these techniques can help raise the probability of successful improvements by providing some structure to improvement efforts. Moreover they helping those involved through practical steps that are individually low risk (and consequently less fearful). The "prize", as in the case of GE Capital mentioned in the quote at the beginning of this chapter, is the ability to embrace change as a foundation for continuous improvement and competitive advantage, as well as reducing the cost of poor quality.

Cost of Poor Quality

Before exploring practical continuous improvement steps, I encourage the reader to reflect on the cost of poor quality in an enterprise that they are familiar with.

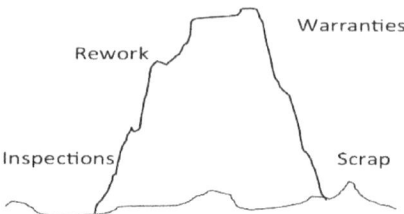

Some costs such as the time taken to conduct inspections, the cost of the people involved, the cost of re-work, scrap and warranty expenses are "visible".

As with the ice in an iceberg, much of the cost of poor quality is "hidden" below the waterline. The likes of set-up costs for re-work, lost sales, poorer customer loyalty, increased volume of "work in progress" and unpredictable costs and revenues are less immediately apparent.

Clients

Can you list the clients for your products / services? I believe strongly that continuous improvement starts with gaining clarity about the clients you have and the "outcomes" they are buying – these can be in the external marketplace or internally within your enterprise. As business has evolved from a world of mass marketing where clients / customers were considered as one group (or perhaps a series of segment groups), to one where technology and data allows us to strive to serve "markets of one", I sense that a critical success factor is understanding the diversity of clients / customers and the variety of outcomes that they are buying.

Please think for a moment about the people or organisations that benefit from the products or services that you and your team provide. I find it helpful to think holistically about this and identify:

- The **suppliers** that "feed" your business activity.
- The **inputs** that the suppliers provide – these may be physical products, services or perhaps data of some kind that you then process.
- The **process** steps you use to transform the inputs.
- The **outcomes** that your customers "buy".

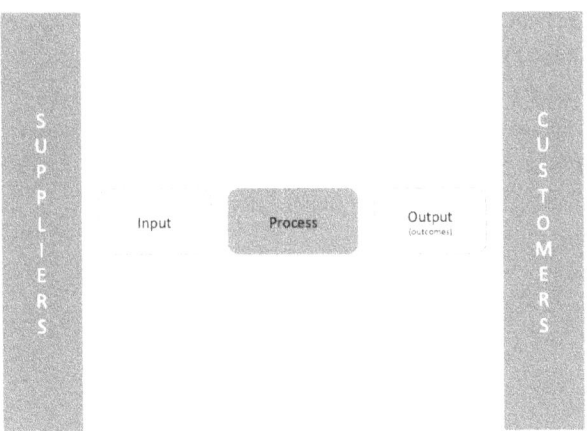

Client Expectations

A theme running through a number of the cost of poor quality factors is a gap between the attributes of the service or product produced and the expectations – of either your own enterprise or your client.

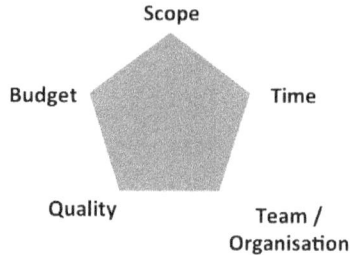

My premise is that a solid understanding of client expectations is the foundation for establishing the "dimensions" of the product or service you are providing. These "dimensions" comprise, scope, cost, timelines, people delivering the product or service and the level of quality.

Managing these dimensions of your offering, in alignment with your client's expectations, provides a foundation for satisfying their requirements. Developing a sufficient understanding of their expectations is of course the challenge. I have developed a habit of making a note of stated expectations during meetings and of asking probing questions to develop a sense of their unstated expectations. Where my delivery team considered an expectation to be unrealistic we would consider alternative approaches that could meet the client need and then discuss these with the Client to seek an agreement to the alternative. Having then confirmed these expectations with the Client, the challenge is to put in place a plan to meet them! I will return to this in the Critical to Quality discussion below.

#	Stakeholder	Expectation	Alternative Expectation (If unrealistic expectations have been gathered think about alternatives that would support a win/win)	Action

I have used a similar expectation gathering approach to help me meet the expectations my own boss had for me. For example, a person I directly reported to but saw rarely (he was based on the other side of the Atlantic ocean), was exceptionally busy but nonetheless had an expectation that I keep him up to date on the issues I was working on. The volume of emails was such that we considered other options. Our conclusion was a mix of concise voicemails that he could listen to when driving to work and instant messages for urgent items.

Critical to Quality

Having established an understanding of the client expectations - their vision of a successful outcome - the next step is to consider the factors that are critical to the quality of meeting each expectation. For example if a client expects that urgent product support questions are answered within 4 hours, it is important for those dealing with support questions to know this, and to put in place a process for meeting this expectation. Following Peter Drucker's [1] observation that "What gets measured gets done", putting in place an appropriate measure and a target would also be prudent. Target setting has in my view elements of both art and science; however, I am always keen to avoid "averages". The client in

---
[1] Perhaps the original Management Guru

this case feels the variation in the time taken to deal with urgent support questions and an average measure may well hide some totally unacceptable performances. In this case I would brainstorm with my team what percentage of urgent support questions they believe could be answered in 4 hours. Depending upon the answer I would then consider whether additional resources may be necessary and if so what the cost implications would be.

A similar approach can be used for addressing the requirements of other stakeholders. For example, in a professional services firm the Partners may have a particular focus on securing prompt payment for the partnership's services. A popular metric used to give this a focus is "Days sales outstanding" (DSO). A critical to quality factor from the partnership perspective may be that DSO on each client account is less than 60.

Periodic reviews of the critical to quality factors with the relevant stakeholders can be a good way of validating whether the enterprise is focusing its resources appropriately. Some year ago I recall reading about an example of a kitchen catering for senior employees in a business. Knowing that the Company Chairman liked steak pies the chef directed that there would always be a steak pie immediately available should the Chairman arrive for lunch. Whilst one could naturally consider this to be a waste of resources, it only surfaced as an issue some years later when a subsequent chef was asked why there was always one steak pie in stock. It transpired that the Chairman had retired a couple of years previously so by no stretch of the imagination could having a steak pie in stock be considered critical to the quality of the service provided by the kitchen!

Critical to Process

Building on the Critical to Quality product support example above, my next step would be identifying the critical to process factors that would need to be met in order to achieve the critical to quality requirement that urgent product support questions are answered within 4 hours. These might include:

a. Logging all support requests within 15 minutes and categorizing those urgent for special handing.
b. Escalating urgent support requests to the appropriate individual within 30 minutes.
c. Escalating any unanswered urgent requests after 3.5 hours.

After considering the critical to process steps required to achieve the performance identified as Critical to Quality, I would review the feasibility of achieving the level of service expected. If this is in doubt I would be keen to have a proactive dialogue with the client - perhaps along the lines of us setting jointly a performance standard that would expect 95% of urgent support requests to be addressed in less than 4 hours. I would then put in place a dashboard to share with the client showing the volume of support requests, the number classified urgent, our performance in meeting the performance standard and a narrative explanation for the urgent requests not met within 4 hours.

Turning to the less than 60 Days Sales Outstanding, that was considered "critical to quality" by the professional services firm Partners. Critical to process steps could include:

a. An explicit term in Client contracts requiring invoices to be paid within 14 days.
b. Identifying the person at the client who approves invoices for payment.
c. All individuals working on client projects reporting the time spent on each project weekly.
d. Monthly invoices being prepared for Client Partner approval on working Day 1 of each month.
e. Approved invoices being submitted to the person responsible for approval on working Day 2 of each month.

Enterprises such as Motorola, GE, Dow and a spectrum of Financial Services have extended this critical to quality and critical to process thinking into a robust implementation of Six Sigma - a quality improvement approach that defines defects and statistically analyses these as a basis for reducing variation in performance. As part of my work as a Director of Operations at Accenture, I used the Six Sigma approach to determine the measures we used to promote continuous improvement of our business development and quality processes and subsequently in our intellectual property company.

Building Quality into Work

Back in 1961 Shigeo Shingo at Toyota implemented a system known as "Poke Yoke" to error proof processes against mistakes. The mistake proofing approach recognized that human beings make mistakes and creates designs and systems that minimise or eliminate these. There are two components:

- Mistake prevention.
- Immediate mistake detection.

When you refuel your car for example, the size of the end of the hose filler reduces the risk of putting fuel with lead into a car requiring unleaded fuel. The filler cap is generally attached to the car to reduce the risk of loss and the cap itself has a click mechanism to reduce the risk of over tightening it.

The National Institute of Standard Technology (NIST) published a study in 2002 noting that the cost of fixing one bug found in the production stage of software is 15 hours compared to five hours of effort if the same bug were found in the coding stage. It is not therefore surprising that software development methodologies include "stage containment" steps that aim to identify errors before development moves to the next stage. A similar approach can be adopted in the development of most products and services. For example, when taking a customer order, having electronic validation that ensures the order quantity is entered and other attributes complete before transmitting the order to the warehouse etc.

Process Sponsorship

Once a clear understanding has been developed of the steps that are critical to the achievement of the quality outcomes (as perceived by the client), four immediate actions are helpful:

1. Appoint an appropriately senior individual to be the "sponsor" of the process involved.

2. Identify who should be accountable, who should be responsible, who should be consulted and who should be informed at each step in the process and who should be responsible for continuous improvement. Note that only one person should be accountable for each step in a process.
3. Under the sponsor's direction undertake an assessment of any barriers to implementation - for example, do any existing policies or procedures need to be amended? Are there any tools (including job aids) that could be developed to help people deliver the quality outcomes efficiently, effectively and consistently? An example of a job aid – designed to provide individuals with the full context of a process - is below.
4. Set a date for reviewing the process to establish whether it remains "fit for purpose" having due regard for changes in the enterprise and its business environment.

An example Job Aid

Purpose:

The XXX accounts payable process facilitates pre-approval of business expenditure within agreed delegations, appropriate approvals of invoices & expenses and payment through BACS.

Process Diagram:

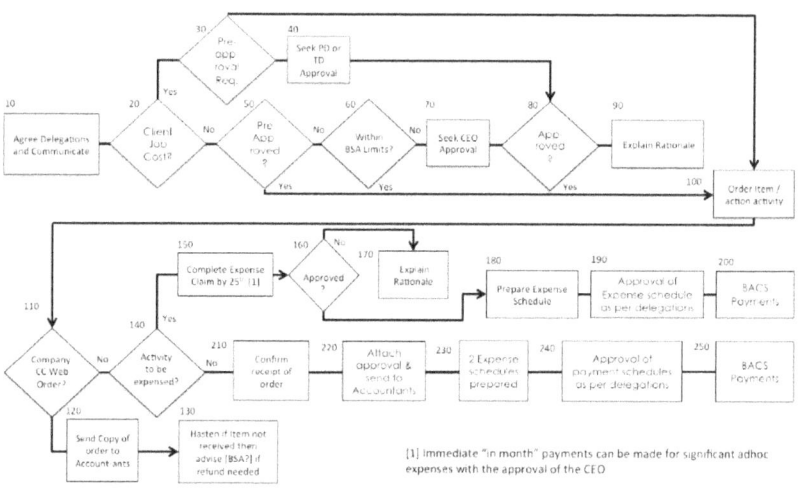

Process Description (A key to appointments is below the table):

[1] Responsible [2] Accountable [3] Consulted [4] Informed

Step	Description	Res(1)	Acc(2)	Con(3)	Inf(4)
10	Discuss, agree & communicate authorities to approve expenses that will be billed & collected from clients, other Client specific costs, Routine General Administrative costs (up to XXX), Staff Expenses.	CEO	CEO	PD, TD, BSA	All
20	Segment costs between those that are related to delivering sold work and other costs.				

STRATTOMICS

Step	Description	Res(1)	Acc(2)	Con (3)	Inf(4)
30	TD and PD set criteria for Pre Approval of job delivery related costs	TD / PD	TD / PD		
40	For Professional Services jobs seek approval of TD for costs related to delivery of client jobs e.g. travel, xxx, xxx. For Software implementations seek approval of PD for implementation related costs.	Requester	TD / PD		
50	Establish whether the Sales or General Administrative cost concerned has already been approved	Requester	CEO	TD / PD	Requester
60	Establish whether the cost concerned can be approved by the BSA	Requester	BSA	TD / PD	Requester
70	Email CEO with request for approval of costs for item / service needed	Requester	BSA	TD / PD	Requester
80	Expenditure request considered	CEO	CEO	TD / PD	Requester
90	If request is not being approved, explain to the requester the reasons	CEO	CEO		Requester
100	Order item (from standard supplier if appropriate) / service, engage in activity (e.g. Travel)	Requester	Requester	CEO	BSA
110	Company Credit Card Order?	Requester	Requester		
120	If Company credit card used, send copy of order to Accountant by email	Requester	Requester		
130	Make a diary reminder to ensure receipt of item / service is confirmed	Requester	Requester		
140	If individual has mileage expenses or personally paid for the item / activity / service it expense as soon as possible	Requester	Requester		

150	Complete the company mileage or expense form by 25th of the month	Reques-ter	Reques-ter		
160	Approval of expense claim in accordance with delegations	TBC	CEO		TD / PD
170	If request is not being approved, explain to the requester the reasons	CEO	CEO		Req-uester
180	Prepare Schedule of approved expenses submitted by staff	BSA	BSA		
190	Approval of expense schedule in accordance with delegations approved by CEO. NOTES: 1. Any novel or in anyway non-standard payments should be approved personally by the CEO. 2. With the exception of the CEO, employees are not authorised to approve payments to themselves.	BSA	BSA CEO	CEO	CEO
200	Make Bank Payment	BSA	CEO		
210	Confirm receipt of item on the invoice or copy of order and pass to the approver	Requester	Requester		BSA
220	Email copy of invoice / order to accountant with approval	App	App		BSA
230	Prepare schedules of payments for approval: A. Payments that can be approved by the BSA by 30th of the month, B. Schedule of all other payments for approval of the CEO by working day zzz of the month	PA	PA	CEO	BSA
240	Approval of payment schedules in accordance with delegations approved by CEO. NOTES: 1. Any novel or in anyway non-standard payments should be approved personally by the CEO. 2. With the exception of the CEO, employees are not authorised to approve	BSA / CEO	CEO	CEO	

STRATTOMICS

	payments to them selves.				
250	Make Bank (BACS) Payment	PA	PA	CEO	CEO

APP	Approver - in accordance with delegations	APP	Approver - in accordance with delegations
BSA	Business Support Administrator	BSA	Business Support Administrator
PA	Accounting	PD	Product Director
PD	Product Director	PEM	Product Engagement Manager

Plan, Do, Check, Act

However well you have designed your activities and endeavoured to build quality into your processes (using the likes of Poke Yoke to minimise mistakes), there is likely to be huge potential for continuous improvement - improvements that should increase the satisfaction of your customers and other. In the 1930s Walter Shewhart, a statistician, developed statistical process control in the Bell Laboratories in the United States of America. Subsequently this thinking was embedded into the Quality movement pioneered by W Edwards Deming in the 1950s. At its core is a Plan, Do, Check, Act (PDCA) cycle – known sometimes as the Deming Wheel.

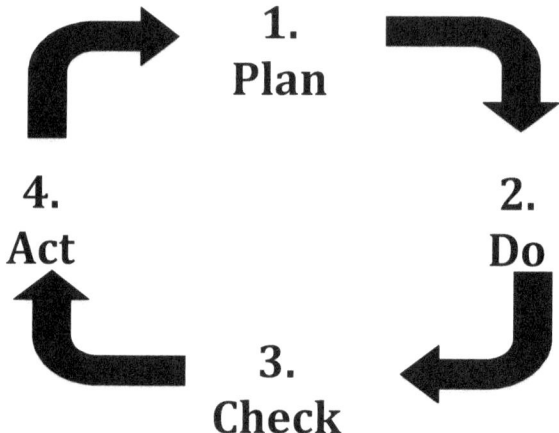

The checking step may include measurements introduced when considering the critical to process factors, identified as central to delivering products or services that meet the quality expectations of customers, or sophisticated statistical process control techniques. After the PDCA cycle has been completed, the "standard" level of performance of the activity concerned should be higher. Over time, repeated PDCA cycles can have a very material impact on the quest to improve enterprise performance.

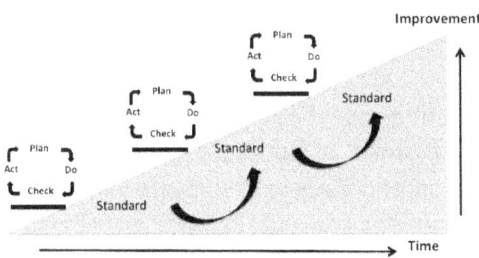

This well-established method has stood the test of time. It is a mandated approach in some organisations – not least as a consequence of quality standards that they may be certified to (For example the old 2005 ISO27001 standard (*Information technology - Security techniques - Information Security Management Systems - Requirements*) mandated it). In my experience a key to securing value from this, and indeed other quality management techniques, is to keep the focus on the "changing needs of the customer" and to avoid building a mass of bureaucracy around the core idea of planning, doing and checking, that can in itself become a barrier to agility.

Identifying the Root cause of performance issues

The "5 Whys" technique can be an effective approach to structuring analysis to identify the root cause of a performance issue. The technique was formalised as part of the Toyota Production System and is now in widespread use as part of Kaizen, Lean manufacturing, Six Sigma and other quality management approaches. For example, a customer for a project to transfer an archive of enterprise data from their servers to a cloud service may raise a complaint. In this case the iterative process of asking 5 questions may establish that:

1. Why - the project running behind schedule.
2. Why - the project team have identified more work than in the original plan.
3. Why – the validation of data prior to transfer to the cloud is failing.
4. Why - many incidents of data corruption have been found.

5. Why – client staff turnover has been high and the individuals currently involved have not been maintaining the servers containing legacy data. This is necessitating collection of back up data from an external back up service provider.

One tool for facilitating robust analysis of root causes is the fishbone or Ishikawa diagram (named after Kaoru Ishikawa who had pioneered quality techniques in the Kawasaki shipyards in Japan). This tool is a favourite of management consultants because it is an effective way of identifying the potential factors causing an overall effect and then communicating these to stakeholders. Causes (reasons for imperfection), are generally segmented according to the source of the variance. For example for an analysis of a manufacturing issue the following segmentation may be appropriate:

- People
- Methods – including procedures
- Machines
- Materials
- Metrics i.e. Data used to evaluate the quality of the process(es) being used
- Environment

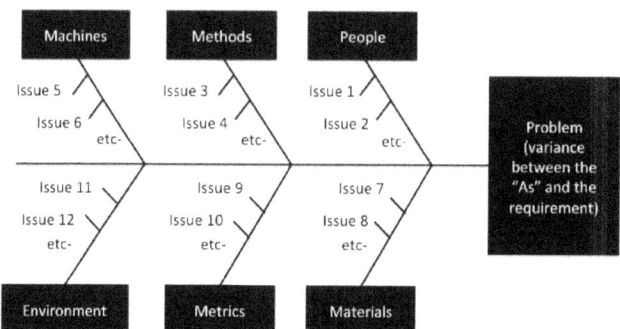

If the issue is in a marketing activity the segmentation could be:

- Product / Service
- Positioning
- Price
- Place
- Promotion
- People
- Packaging

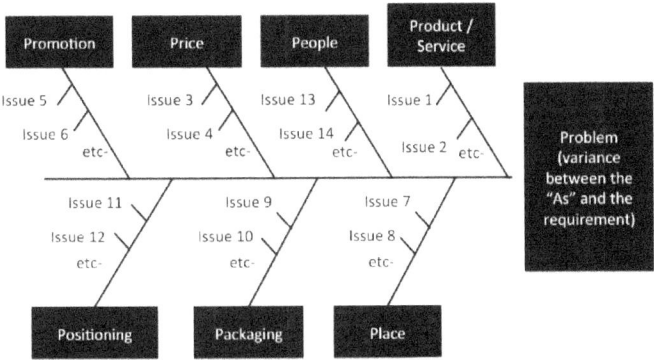

Initiating changes

Having identified the root cause of the problem i.e. the variance between the "As Is" and the level of performance required to meet customer expectations, an action(s) will need to be initiated to close the gap. Before deciding on the action(s) consideration of factors that will impact on the change can help you shape and position the actions needed to implement the change in a way that implementation is more likely to be successful. In this section I will introduce a further 3 tools to your toolbox that can help you shape and prioritise improvement actions:

- Force Field Analysis
- Effective / Attainable Analysis
- Importance / Performance Matrix

Force Field Analysis

Kurt Lewin of the University of Iowa, one of the early writers on Change Management, suggested that it is helpful to think about the propagators (driving forces) and inhibitors (blockers) of change when shaping actions – on the basis that building on the driving forces alone will generally increase the inhibitors of change. He termed this "Force Field Analysis".

You can implement a Force Field Analysis using the following steps:

1. Define the outcome of the change in a short statement.
2. List the personal, interpersonal, inter-group, cultural, administrative, technological and environmental (and any other) factors that will drive the change needed to achieve the outcome
3. List the personal, interpersonal, inter-group, cultural, administrative, technological, environmental (and any other) factors that will restrain the change needed to achieve the outcome
4. Consider each of these forces in turn to identify how influential / strong each one is. How much if any control do you have over each of the forces? Are there connections between the forces i.e. if you influenced one would it affect another?
5. Rank those that you can influence in order of importance
6. Identify practical actions you could take that will:
    a. Build on driving forces.
    b. Reduce resisting forces.

For example you may face the following in an opportunity to expand the scope of services you supply to a public sector client:

STRATTOMICS

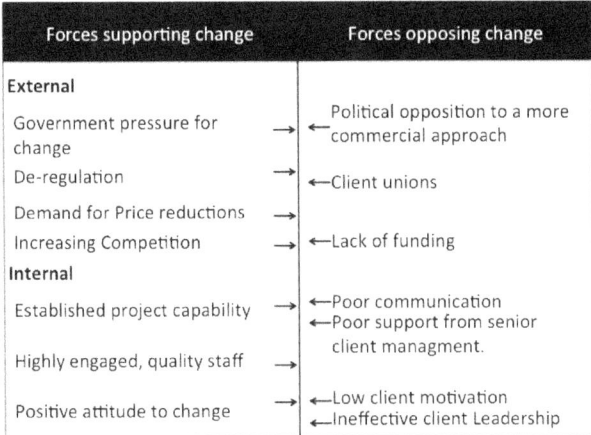

Following a conversation where the age and reliability of the current file storage is mentioned as a major concern, you decide to produce a proposal to provide the client with cloud based file storage. A "brainstorming" workshop with your colleagues highlights the following assessment of "driving forces" and "blockers":

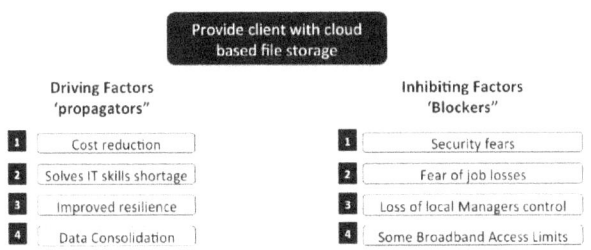

Following further internal discussion you decide on the following tactics to exploit the "driving forces" while addressing the "blockers":

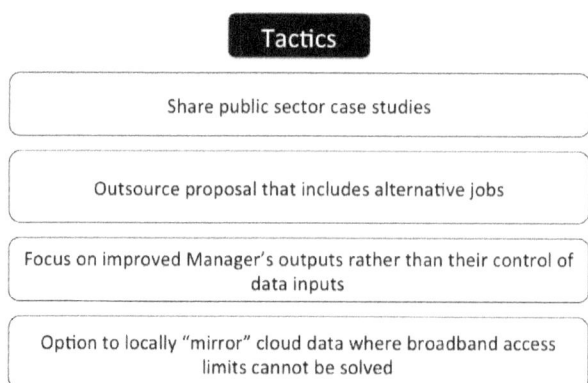

Effective / Attainable Analysis

When considering how to address business improvement opportunities, more than one option is usually identified. Before conducting some form of financial cost benefit analysis it can be helpful to rank the options on the basis of effectiveness and attainability.

For example, in an enterprise I used to work with, the time taken for clients to pay invoices was increasing and this increase in receivables from clients was both hurting cash flow and increasing operational costs (the enterprise used Economic Value Added as one of the key measures of organisational performance and optimising free cash flow was a priority). The following options for reducing client receivables were tabled in a discussion amongst the Leadership Team:

- A. Advance bill clients for our services (with a modest discount for prompt payment).
- B. Reduce the time taken to issue invoices.
- C. Hand-deliver invoices to the person responsible for approving them for payment and invite them to highlight immediately any issues they have with the invoice.
- D. Hasten overdue invoices more frequently and escalate non-payment earlier for follow up by more senior staff.
- E. Stop work on projects where invoices are overdue.

F. Reduce payment terms on new engagements from 30 days to 14 days.

Following the discussion, the Chief Financial Officer (CFO) assessed the effectiveness of each of the suggestions as follows:

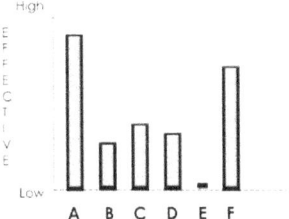

The CFO then had telephone conversations with three of the most experienced Account Managers and debated the attainability of each of the suggestions. The conclusion was:

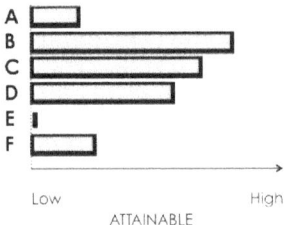

Prior to the following Executive meeting the CFO circulated the following matrix to provoke further discussion and a decision.

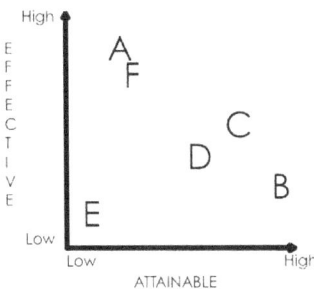

The Executive Team decided to:

1. Build an advanced billing option into all new proposals.
2. Reduce standard payment terms to 14 days.
3. Hand-deliver invoices to the person responsible for approving them for payment and invite them to highlight immediately any issues they had with the invoice.
4. Hasten overdue invoices more frequently and escalate non-payment earlier for follow-up by more senior staff.

Over the following year these actions had a material impact on improving the enterprise's free cash flow.

Importance Performance Matrix

In addition to considering the effectiveness and attainability of an improvement from the perspective of one's own enterprise, it is prudent to consider it from the perspective of the customer(s).

Returning to the example used earlier in the Critical to Quality discussion[2] a proposal to introduce an automated "ticketing" system for support questions could be assessed on the basis of effectiveness and client satisfaction. I would approach this by:

1. Identifying the attributes of the solution that will impact the satisfaction of the customer's Critical to Quality (CTQ) factors. If there were any doubts about this I would seek a conversation with the customer - the last thing I would want, is to surprise an important customer with a change in our processes without any consultation! For example, does the customer value having on-line access to the status of their support questions?
2. Consider how important each of these attributes is to the Customer.
3. Assess how effectively you can satisfy the most important attribute.
4. Chart your assessment on an Importance - Performance Matrix showing the customer's satisfaction and your anticipated effectiveness in satisfying it.

---

[2] A customer who expects that urgent product support questions are answered by your enterprise within 4 hours.

For example, the client may value being able to see immediately on a web page, details of support calls not being cleared after 3 hours. The proposed "ticketing" system could easily provide this visibility without adding to your costs so:

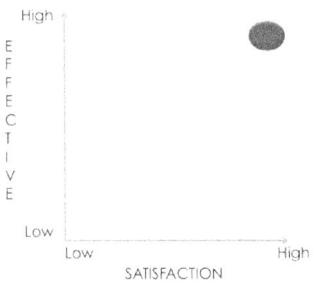

In one organisation where I implemented this, an unexpected benefit was realised. The client identified a number of unresolved calls that he considered were not urgent and "counselled his staff" to only categorise as urgent the issues that impacted their ability to satisfy their clients. This is a good example of improving both effectiveness and efficiency by "giving visibility" to data that might usually be hidden in systems or on people's desks.

Balancing efficiency and innovation

As enterprises strive to improve the quality of the services and products that they supply to their clients / customers today, inevitable tensions will arise with the work necessary to develop new opportunities. A challenge for leaders is to legitimise both the delivery and improvement of current offerings and the time and expense necessary to develop the next generation of enterprise offerings. Some describe this as Organisational ambidexterity[3] - "The capability to exploit existing competencies and explore new opportunities".

---

[3] Tushman & O'Reilly, "Ambidextrous organizations: Managing evolutionary and revolutionary change", 1996

Conclusion

I hope that the techniques that I have introduced in this chapter are useful additions to your enterprise management "tool box" and that they will help your institutionalise continuous improvement into your enterprise DNA. Moreover, I hope that using these techniques - in an agile way - will raise the ability of your enterprise to embrace change as a foundation for continuous improvement and competitive advantage and serve as a launch pad for strategies and tactics to enhance future performance.

> "Good evidence now exists that, there is a body of management practices which is strongly associated with better performance regardless of time or place"
>
> The Economist, 18 January 2014

Please activate the QR code below (or type http://wp.me/P3ep12-sY into your browser) to reach a web page containing a number of templates and useful links to further information.

3 RAISING AGILITY

> *"In turbulent markets, organizational agility, which I define as the capacity to identify and capture opportunities more quickly than rivals do, is invaluable. Executives know this: a recent McKinsey survey found that nine out of ten executives ranked organizational agility both as critical to business success and as growing in importance over time.[2] The benefits of enhanced agility, according to survey respondents, include higher revenues, more satisfied customers and employees, improved operational efficiency, and a faster time to market."*
>
> McKinsey Quarterly "Competing through Organizational Agility"

The primary purpose of this Chapter is to inspire broader thinking about the future of your enterprise, as a platform for raising your organisational agility. Some of the well-established frameworks and tools discussed have been foundations for the extensive work done by Corporate Planning departments in the past; however, my objective is not to persuade you to allocate resources to huge annual planning efforts but rather to use the frameworks to help you develop insights on changes in your marketplace - on a continuous basis. For example, when people started spending more on smartphones and mobile phone company charges, was there a correlation with less spending on other leisure activities? Perhaps socialising in local pubs or gym memberships would fall as people needed to make economies to pay for their

Smartphones? In other words was the virtual networking available through the Smartphone a substitute for meeting people in pubs and fitness clubs? If you own a fitness club and are armed with this insight can you develop services that turn the Smartphone into something that augments your fitness club rather than becomes a substitute for membership?

Effective strategic thinking has a laser like beam, penetrating all the way from the mission through to initiatives that grow enterprise capabilities (with measures and targets) to address the needs of customers, employees and other stakeholders. As you think about this, a good discipline is to look through the "lens" of a spectrum of the customers for the enterprise's products and services and then the "lens" of other stakeholders:

- What does success look like for each of these constituencies?
- What developments are there in the market place that may influence these views of success?

The first part of this chapter is designed to help you maintain a broad understanding of your market, so that opportunities to innovate or capture market share are more apparent. Your capability to anticipate and sense changes consequently increases. Subsequently I will discuss how enterprises can develop more efficient, effective and consistent reflexes so these opportunities are exploited.

How agile is your Enterprise?

The following 12 questions were posed in an Accenture Outlook Journal article[4]. Please answer the questions as a start point for thinking further about business agility.

1. Does your organisation have at least three scenarios for how your industry is most likely to evolve over the next 36 months? Does it have good options for responding?
2. What three big opportunities would your company be pursuing if it were more agile?
3. Imagine three possible sources of competition that you haven't thought about until now. How will you respond to them?

---

[4] Accenture Outlook Journal, No 3 of 2012

4. Put yourself in your top competitors' shoes. What could they do to disrupt the market in the next year, and what are your plans for outsmarting them?
5. How is your company augmenting its ability to quickly sense new market anomalies? Are you taking full advantage of the new capabilities of today's analytics tools?
6. What are the three biggest factors preventing your organisation from becoming more agile? How do you plan to overcome them?
7. Did you make such big cuts during the recession (particularly in terms of talent) that your agility and ability to grow have been damaged? If so, how are you compensating now for those cuts?
8. In what areas should you be collaborating with competitors to drive change sin the market?
9. Who among your organization's new leaders will be most effective at taking advantage of volatility? What makes them different from your long-time leaders?
10. Which of your competitors are the best leading indicators of future market opportunities?
11. Where would faster decision-making be of most benefit to your company?
12. Have you been able to cut your company's fixed costs in the past few years to improve its agility?

Accenture Outlook Journal, No 3 of 2012

I hope that the spectrum of frameworks, tools and techniques in this Chapter will help you develop actions to address areas of both weakness and opportunity that you have identified in your answers to this questionnaire.

Assessing your "As Is"

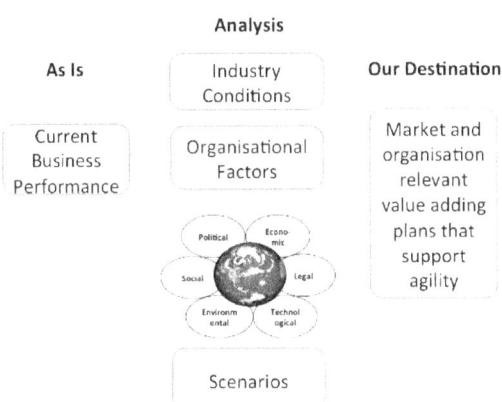

The start point for our journey is an assessment of your current business performance. We will then consider industry conditions and broader issues in your competitive environment before stretching towards our "destination" - a broader understanding that will enable you to develop value-adding plans that help anticipate, sense, respond and adapt to the changing business conditions - with agility.

Current Financial Performance

In general, the financial performance of enterprises follows an "S" curve as revenues start slowly and then accelerated as the demand for the Enterprise's products or services grow. Then as the market matures, and competition increases, revenue growth decreases. As substitute products or services appear, or the underlying customer need disappears, revenues then go into decline.

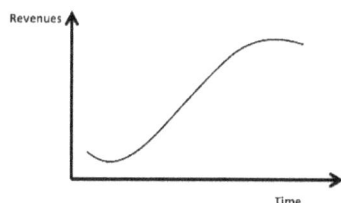

If the growth in your revenues is slowing, ask why?

- Perhaps the market for your product / service is now saturated,
- Is there a new competitor,
- Have the prices, or the positioning of your products in relation to those of your competitors changed,
- Have there been changes in your Enterprise such as changes in your sales force that have subdued growth?

As you read through this chapter please use the tools and frameworks mentioned to generate potential explanations for where your Enterprise is on your financial "S curve" and to anticipate where you are going to be in one, two and three years time.

Applying the same "S curve" thinking, it can be insightful to consider how the distinctiveness of your capabilities evolves over time.

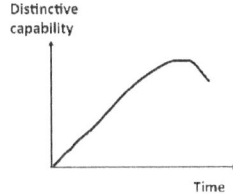

As you develop a new novel idea and build capabilities around it, the distinctiveness of your capabilities grow. Unless you have strong intellectual property protection (i.e. a patent) it is likely that your commercial success will have acted as a magnet for others to come into your market place with offerings that meet the same or similar customer needs. Unless you are able to innovate to continuous bring new value adding features to your product or service it is likely that the distinctiveness of your capabilities will decline. This may well be a leading indicator of a slow down in revenue growth (or at least profitability).

For example, in the early days of cloud services in the information systems arena, enterprises could develop distinctive positions in the marketplace and grow quickly. As larger enterprises like Amazon and Oracle entered the market as it became more mature, the small enterprises that continued to innovate could extend the period where their distinctive capability was a competitive advantage over the large global information systems enterprises.

Analysing Your Marketplace

Effective strategic analysis should expand your thinking and reduce the temptation to plan only from what you already know! Andrew Pettigrew, a Strategy Professor with an anthropological background, of the Said Business School studied the politics of strategic decision[5] some years ago and was fascinated by the inertial properties of organisations. He showed that organisations frequently hold on to faulty assumptions about their world for as long as a decade despite overwhelming

---

[5] Pettigrew, Andrew M, "The Politics of organizational decision-making", 1973.

evidence that it has changed and that they should change too. In our rapidly changing world the capability to sense necessary changes earlier than your competitors can be the foundation for the nimbleness that can be the source of huge benefits for your stakeholders.

The more I have seen of traditional SWOT (Strengths, Weaknesses, Opportunities and Threats) analysis (even when turned around to TOWS to focus on the external factors first), the less value I have sensed in the exercise. Fortunately there is another well-established approach. Drawing on Industrial Organisation theory from Economics, Michael Porter of the Harvard Business School developed a 5-force framework to assess the competitive intensity of a market. The underlying assumption being that the more intense the competition, the less profitable the market will be. The Porter 5-force framework considers:

- Three "horizontal" influences – the threat of new entrants to the market, the threat of substitute products and the competitive rivalry amongst the enterprises competing in a given market.
- Two "vertical" influences – the power of buyers of your product / service and the power of sellers of the inputs you need to produce your product or service.

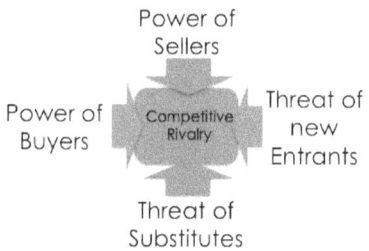

To begin to develop a sense for how these are likely to evolve over time another traditional analysis framework can be informative. Having a "brainstorming session" with colleagues - perhaps facilitated by an individual from outside your enterprise - to consider how factors in the political, economic, legal, social, technological and broader environment (PESTLE) will impact your enterprise in the next 3 years can be a good start. Ideally this discussion can then be extended to include perspectives from your suppliers, alliance partners, customers and a broad spectrum of your employees. In Chapter 4 we will discuss an approach to securing the latter using an Excellence Audit ™ from the Tom Peters Company.

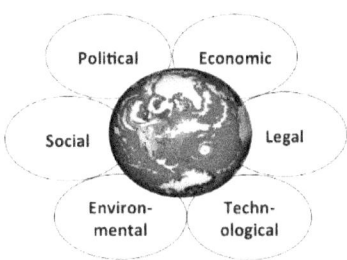

For example the growing impact of social media can have quite profound impacts on enterprises. I recall an enterprise where any form of external communication required clearance by a raft of individuals across the corporate functions - including legal and brand. The time taken to do this would extend to many days if not weeks. Contrast this with the expectations of customers using Twitter. "The moment of value", for an enterprise quoted in a Tweet to engage in dialogue, is perhaps one hour at most. What does this mean for delegating, empowering and developing relatively junior people in enterprises to respond to tweets?

The constant innovation facilitated by technological advances is a broader cause of a further compression of response time. In their book "Big Bang Disruption: Business Survival in the Age of Constant Innovation", Larry Downes and Paul Nunes included a question from Ernest Hemingway's book "The Sun Also Rises" – "How did you go bankrupt?" "Two ways. Gradually and then suddenly." Our discussion earlier of the S curve will hopefully have sensitized you to the value of identifying forces that are slowly impacting the performance of your business. In certain cases, particularly where there is great technological innovation, we need to be alert to the potential for incumbent enterprises to be more prone to rapid destruction by new entrants. For example the manufacturers of portable CD players when flash memory based music players appeared. The potential impact of regulation can also usefully be considered. For example, if the European Union (EU) enacts legislation that requires all corporate data originated in the EU to be maintained on servers in the EU, what would be the impact on public Cloud IT offerings from the likes of Amazon, Google, Microsoft and Oracle?

All the PESTLE dimensions can be drivers of material change in your competitive potential and the underlying economics of your business. Proactively addressing these by making adjustments to your business will improve the likelihood of continuing to achieve your profit and other stakeholder objectives.

7-S Analysis

Another well-established framework that is helpful in thinking about both an enterprise "As Is" and business improvement actions is the "7-S" - developed by Tom Peters, Rob Waterman, Julian Phillips and Anthony Athos [6]. The research that spurred the framework included both primary research conducted at a broad spectrum of enterprises and academic institutions across the planet and consideration of established management literature. The following assertion made in the earlier days of management research by Chester Barnard[7] and highlighted when the framework was originally published[8], resonates ever more powerfully today in our world of social media."

> "The CEO's role is to harness the social forces in the organisation, to shape and guide values …… good value-shapers are effective managers (in contrast with mere manipulators of formal rewards who deal only with the narrower concept of efficiency)"
>
> *Chester Barnard*

The framework was a key component of "In Search of Excellence" – the classic management book subsequently authored by Tom Peters and Rob Waterman[9].

---

[6] Peters. T, Phillips, J. Watermann. R, "Structure is not Organization", Business Horizons, June 1980
[7] Barnard, Chester Irving, "The functions of the executive", 1938.
[8] Peters. T, Phillips, J. Watermann. R, "Structure is not Organization", Business Horizons, June 1980
[9] Peters, Tom & Watermann, Robert, "In Search of Excellence", 1982

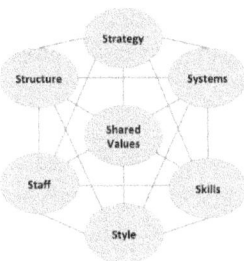

The underlying thinking emphasises that effective enterprises are a consequence of more than purely great strategy and appropriate structure. For example, an enterprise with strong shared values "in its DNA" can be expected to be better able to make appropriate decisions at more junior levels - reducing "the burden" on the senior leaders who have limited capacity to process information. This challenge is going to be ever more apparent in our agile world, where "Big Data" surfaces ever more potential insight, and our volatile marketplaces necessitate faster responses. Fundamental to understanding and applying the "7 S" is an appreciation of both the 7 "variables" and the interconnections. A programme of actions to improve organisational effectiveness should address both. Tom Peters has emphasised that the "real energy required to re-direct an institution comes when all the variables in the model are aligned."

> "I continue to say, over 30 years later, that the power of the 7-Ss and In Search of Excellence (1982) and my subsequent work can best be captured in six words: "Hard is soft. Soft is hard." That is, it's the plans and the numbers that are often "soft" (e.g., the sky-high soundness scores that the ratings agencies gave packages of dubious mortgages). And the people ("staff") and shared values ("corporate culture") and skills ("core competencies" these days) which are truly "hard"—that is, the bedrock upon which the adaptive and enduring enterprise is built. To state the obvious, we very much included the "Hard Ss" (Strategy, Structure, Systems) in our framework, then added the "Soft Ss" (Style, Staff, Skills, Shared values—or Superordinate goal); and insisted that there was no precedence among them. Deal with all seven or accept the consequences—likely less than effective implementation of any project or program or increase in overall organization performance."
>
> Tom Peters

The current Tom Peters "Future Shape of the Winner" takes this a stage further by using a Gyroscope as a metaphor that embeds the essential requirement of maintaining alignment as the overall enterprise moves (potentially at high speed in our agile world). This will be discussed further in the next chapter.

Before examining each of the 7-S "variables" in turn, I should stress that there is no hierarchy amongst the 7 variables and they have no specific order - the driving force amongst the 7 factors, if any, is likely to be specific to a particular enterprise and its current context.

Shared Values (Superordinate Goals):

Values represent the core priorities in the organisation's culture, including what drives members' priorities and how they truly act in the organisation, etc. I have consequently elected to start my description of the 7-S factors with the shared values – or superordinate goals as they were originally described. These are the set of values and aspirations (often unwritten) that are fundamental ideas upon which the enterprise is built. They include an idea of the future strategic direction that top management believe should form part of the enterprise DNA. In top performing enterprises these superordinate goals are communicated concisely, right through the organisation, in ways that carry a rich meaning for the people involved. Reflecting on my 20 years in professional services organisations I can recall enterprises where such superordinate goals (for example Best People) were really lived and other cases where such superordinate goals did not exist.

The entrepreneurs, who initially establish new enterprises, are generally driven by a set of values and in the initial stages of development their enterprise reflects these. As enterprises scale it is increasingly hard to ensure that these values are lived by the employees, and continue to be a guide for individual's behaviour, decision making, and resource allocation etc. That said, I believe the larger the organisation, the more important it is for values to be institutionalised! Values are increasingly important in developing strategies and tactics as they often drive the intent and direction for enterprise leaders - in our agile world where more and more "empowerment" is needed to junior levels in an organisation - these need to be effectively shared. A good understanding of values, and consistent "living' of these values, reduces enterprise risk, minimises the need for complex manuals and other policy documents and, most importantly, increases employee engagement. Engagement of employees and other stakeholders will be a subject I return to in Chapter four.

Effective values based leadership can also be an effective approach to tackling the increasing evidence of a lack of trust in Leadership. The World Economic Forum 2014[10] survey, for example, included "A lack of values in leadership" in the list of top concerns. The Edelman Trust Barometer[11] showed that less than 50% of business leaders are trusted in 16 of 23 markets surveyed in 2013. The latter report headlined a "Crisis of Leadership", with trust in Business Leaders ethics and morality being very low; moreover, very material gaps were highlighted between individual perceptions of organisations and their perceptions of the organisations' leaders.

It can be helpful for enterprises to develop a values statement[12], but for this to be valuable, the process used needs to respect the local cultural norms. The development of a values statement is most effective when a spectrum of methods are used, ranging from highly analytical and rational to highly creative and divergent, to arrive at a description that really captures the organisational values of the enterprise. As the work to develop a values statement progresses, it is important to identify any differences between the organisation's preferred values and its true values (the values actually reflected by members' behaviours in the organisation). One approach to doing this is to record each preferred value on a flash card, then have each employee "rank" the values with 1, 2, or 3 in terms of the priority needed by the organisation with 3 indicating the value is very important to the organisation and 1 is least important. Then go through the cards again to rank how people think the values are actually being enacted in the organisation with 3 indicating the values are fully enacted and 1 indicating the value is hardly reflected at all. The discrepancies where a value is highly preferred (ranked with a 3), but hardly enacted (ranked with a 1) can then form the basis for a programme of initiatives to close the gaps.

---

[10] http://www.weforum.org/reports/outlook-global-agenda-2014
[11] http://www.edelman.com/insights/intellectual-property/trust-2013/
[12] For example, the following is part of a values statement for a plastics company: "We are strategically entrepreneurial in the pursuit of excellence, encouraging original thought and its application, and willing to take risks based on sound business judgment."

Once a values statement is agreed it should be communicated to all staff and new joiners (in ways that show top management commitment to the values). It can then be a platform for actions to align actual behaviour with preferred behaviours and inform the decisions on future strategies and tactics. During my days at Andersen Consulting, significant effort was put into explaining the organisation's six core values to new joiners and to employees at key milestones in their career development - for example at the New Manager School. Values were mentioned as a matter of routine in management discussions and in a broad spectrum of internal communications. I sensed that they were institutionalised into the way we did business from the top to the bottom of the organisation. As I reflect, I draw a stark contrast with my memory of values development in a subsequent organisation. There, marketing "sponsored" a project to develop a values statement. The project drew on the skills of external consultants and included workshops with a broad spectrum of employees. The outputs of the project included an impressive brochure, additional questions on values in annual appraisals and a commitment to probe individual's values during the recruitment processes. The Board enthusiastically endorsed the work done; however, I could not sense real alignment between Board behaviour and the values! Moreover, our highly educated workforce could see it!

Values driven actions

Much has been written about Leaders and Values. One of the new-year blogs in 2014 that particularly resonated with me was from Dr Rick Brickman[13] who commented that top reasons people set goals and don't achieve them is either they haven't clarified values or don't have a specific enough plan."

I would go further and argue that a holistic "values-driven" approach that cascades from Mission and Values through vision, goals, objectives, to initiatives, measures and targets sets a foundation for effectiveness - by transparently linking the efforts you need from your employees and stakeholders to the strategic imperatives of the enterprise.

---

[13] http://www.rickbrinkman.com

In closing this discussion of values, I should include a "health warning". Whilst I am convinced that enterprises that consistently draw on their values to inform their responses to changes in both their external and internal environments have a higher probability of long term success, I am also sensitive to the risk of the set of values in an enterprise clouding the ability to sense changes. Therefore as one applies strategic tools such as Porter Five Force analysis and the 7-S it is valuable to check ones thinking by asking how other enterprises and start-ups would interpret the emerging changes in the competitive environment that you have identified.

Structure

The building blocks of structure are tasks and coordination. Tasks are broken down into components that can be efficiently actioned by some form of specialist and then reintegrated by a coordinating mechanism of some kind. For example, individuals may record the time they spend on a particular project (each individual working on the project is the best specialised "expert" on where his or her time is being spent). Then a coordinating mechanism (an invoice clerk) brings together the details of all the time spent on a particular project and any associated expenses, together with the client's details, and raises the invoice. At a certain size and complexity the task may need to be delegated to a division to retain a maintainable span of control (the traditional answer) or passed to some form of shared service centre where additional coordination (potentially processes and technology) are applied to enable larger scale operations to be delivered effectively and efficiently. Historically enterprises naturally split tasks by function (for example, Finance, Legal, Human Resources, Marketing etc.), product or perhaps geographic dimensions; however, with the rapid expansion of matrix type organisations the potential for duplication, and ever more difficult coordination, mushroomed. This was an important context for the Business Process Re-engineering movement of the 1990s. This included the move to enterprise processes having process owners responsible for cross-function, cross-geography etc. etc. effectiveness and the process improvement activities outlined in the last chapter. One trend that is particularly apparent in High Performing enterprises is the widespread use of project teams to achieve specific, time bound, strategic tasks that are disbanded as soon as the task is delivered.

Strategy:

> *"Strategy is the way a company aims to improve its position vis a vis competition."*
>
> *Waterman, Peters & Phillips*[14]

Alfred Chandler, another of the "fathers" of management books[15], pointed out that a strategy of diversity, forces a decentralized structure (structure follows strategy). Whilst there are robust examples of companies that have developed and evolved strategies that have been effective over time, have aligned structures and strong shared values[16], there are very many enterprises with well thought strategies, aligned structures and shared values that have not been successful. Consideration of the remaining 4 "Ss" can provide insights on the drivers of such success or failure.

Systems:

How does an enterprise get things done? All the formal and informal procedures, job aids and processes, as well as the spectrum of information / computer applications, that enable enterprises to get things done comprise "systems" in the 7-S framework. A mix of continuous improvement and well-sponsored capability improvement

---

[14] Peters. T, Phillips, J. Watermann. R, "Structure is not Organization", Business Horizons, June 1980
[15] Chandler, Alfred D., "Strategy and Structure: Chapters in the History of the American Industrial Enterprise", 1962
[16] for example GE that I quoted at the beginning of the continuous improvement chapter and Innocent drinks - launched in the UK in 1999 and acquired by Coca Cola in 2013

projects can have a huge impact on the effectiveness of an organisation - without the disruptive side effects that can flow from restructuring initiatives. On the other hand, if the systems in an enterprise cannot generate efficiently the data needed to implement a new strategy then, at best, huge expense on resources will be needed to develop 'workarounds" and temporary "fixes". For example, an enterprise I was familiar with generated the bulk of its revenues in the United States. Following the acquisition of another company, a cost reduction strategy was put in place that included consolidating the accounting onto one system. The system chosen had proved reliable and fit for purpose for the US business and a small volume of European projects. Following the acquisition there was a materially higher volume of projects across Europe and the accounting system required, what amounted to manual actions, to complete the accounting actions for these projects. As a result, additional finance personnel were needed, the Leadership Team's management information was delayed and uncertainty over the accuracy of manual interventions proved a distraction - one that diverted leadership attention from the external marketplace.

Style:

Variables under the 7-S style category include how managers choose to spend their time and their approach to interacting with others. Some top executives signal in quite a collaborative way what is on their mind (perhaps using Twitter or other social media) - reinforcing messages, nudging people in a particular direction- whilst others may adopt a traditional command and control style. The former may do this naturally, using up very little of the time in their hectic schedules. Others may spend much more time working on repeated drafts of formal updates, that are subject to clearance by all the functional heads (Finance, HR, Legal, Marketing etc.), before circulation, and limiting their capacity to give "Top Management Attention" to anticipating and sensing emerging issues.

I am seeing more and more written about the values of leaders being seen and perceived as authentic. Foundations for achieving this in my view include:

- Physical and virtual management by walking about (so that leaders are not only seen but also have the benefit of "unsandpapered" assessments from their employees and other stakeholders - rather than purely commentary from Enterprise Head Office). I have personally seen the value of this while working for a Commander in Chief in the Royal Air Force - the dialogues I witnessed were invaluable in helping the Commander-in-Chief anticipate and sense changes and for individuals at all levels in the organisation to hear first hand perspectives on new capabilities and emerging requirements. The Commander-in-Chief concerned had a most engaging style, that made this easier to do authentically than perhaps would have been the case for some of his colleagues.

- Aligning leadership style, consistently, with the organisational structure, strategy, shared values (and indeed the other 7-S factors) – recognising the evolving needs of the modern enterprise:

"I imagine the modern organisation as a three-dimensional hollow cube. The leader of today sits in the centre of the cube and, scattered around all six sides, are the product, geographic and functional entities that comprise the global corporation. Some of these are closer, emotionally and physically, to the CEO, while others are more remote. Within this complex hollow cube, the CEO can no longer hope to issue orders and to see them faithfully carried out. Indeed, all he or she can do is to exercise influence and steer this writhing disparate mass of employees, customers, products and technologies towards the desired vision for the global business.

Iain Martin 2013[17]

While an Associate Partner at Accenture I witnessed the change in one operating group when a new, very energetic, "hands-on", Group CEO was appointed. She personally, and very visibly, sponsored a range of growth initiatives and provided 'top cover' for individuals to try new things with clients so that we built a spectrum of new capabilities to replace the large historic systems development projects that had been the backbone of the group's work.

Style, from a 7-S perspective also embraces an Enterprise's culture. The dissertation I completed as part of my MBA, investigated the New

---

[17] http://www.ijmartin.com/noticeboard/

Management Strategy in the Ministry of Defence and concluded that effective implementation of the strategy necessitated a culture change and that this was going to take time!

Staff:

Three questions:

- How do you develop your first line supervisors, your managers and the people you believe have the capability of being your future leaders (or do you endeavour to "buy-in" skills as you need them)?
- How do your leading competitors develop their first line supervisors, managers and the people they believe have the capability of being their future leaders?
- How do you shape the basic values of your management team?

The original Peters, Waterman and Phillips research[18] highlighted that superbly organised companies pay extraordinary attention to managing a process to socialise new recruits into their enterprises, manage their careers and develop them into future managers. These processes include mechanisms to provide mentoring and counselling, well-orchestrated opportunities for access to top management and openings to participate in project teams. During my time at Accenture, in addition to having well structured induction programmes and actively engaged career counsellors, we devoted serious top management effort to teaching our points of view on business issues / developments / challenges to more junior staff. Moreover, one of the four criteria for annual assessments, was the development of people. Google consider individuals potential for two, three or four roles in the future when recruiting because they believe it is essential to recruit individuals who have the personal capability to grow with the rapidly expanding company. In the Royal Air Force, Officers Annual Appraisals included an assessment of each individual's potential to be promoted two ranks higher. How do you approach the recruitment and development of your people?

---

[18] Peters. T, Phillips. J, Watermann. R, "Structure is not Organization", Business Horizons, June 1980

To quote Peters, Waterman and Phillips[19]:

> "Considering people as a pool of resources to be nurtured, developed, guarded and allocated is one of the many ways to turn the "staff" dimension of our 7-S framework into something not only amenable to, but worthy of practical control by senior management."

Skills

Three questions:

- What does your enterprise do best?
- What are the crucial attributes of your enterprise that enable you to deliver at your best today?
- What are the crucial attributes of your enterprise that will enable you to deliver at your best in 24 months time?

In our agile world enterprises are increasingly frequently facing discontinuities in business conditions, that necessitate more than a change in the strategic or tactical focus of their people, and other resources. To evolve the enterprise to address the needs of the changing market place, new capabilities are frequently going to be needed, and currently embedded skills may no longer be needed.

For example, in the Information Systems arena, the emergence of cloud services as a robust business alternative to running servers and their associated software "in-house", creates great opportunities for service providers in the short-term to transition enterprises off their "in-house" systems. The skills developed in doing this may well become redundant as the wave of cloud transitions fades. A challenge for enterprises in this space will be to re-skill / up-skill their people to be relevant to the next wave of demand. Perhaps with Business analytics skills to exploit the colossal opportunities of ever-growing "big data", as more and more devices connect to the Internet?

To conclude this discussion of the 7-S framework, I would like to leave you with the following thoughts.

---

[19] Peters. T, Phillips, J. Watermann. R, "Structure is not Organization", Business Horizons, June 1980

- Firstly, this framework is tried and tested and is not this year's fad!
- Secondly, it is the framework that I have found most applicable to the task of seeking to understand how an enterprise really works.
- Thirdly, it provides a holistic basis for developing a broad scope of coordinated actions - actions that can improve the probability of successfully growing an enterprise. Done well, this builds the agility necessary in our rapidly changing world to capitalise on ever more discontinuities.

Scenarios

One technique, that can help further inform your senses on developments in the market place, is scenario planning. Some enterprises, such as Shell have invested huge effort to generate very sophisticated scenarios; however, a very modest investment of time, and most importantly strategic thinking, can help leadership teams form actionable views on the shape of their marketplace in future. For example:

1. Select several forces and imagine related changes that could influence your enterprise. For example an aging population, efforts by global industry enterprises to penetrate your small and medium sized business market, or a significant competitor poaching your key staff. Scanning the business press and social media for key headlines often suggests potential changes that might impact the enterprise.
2. For each change in a force, discuss three different future scenarios (including best case, worst case, and highest probability / mid case) that could impact the enterprise as a result of each change. Debating the worst-case scenario often provokes a readiness to consider changing / evolving the strategic direction of the enterprise.
3. Suggest potential strategies / tactics the enterprise could adopt, in each of the three scenarios, to respond to each change.

4. Select the highest probability changes, that could have the greatest impact on the enterprise over the next three to five years. Then identify the most appropriate strategies the enterprise could undertake to exploit / mitigate the changes.

The following template can help you implement this technique:

Forces driving External Change	Impact of External Force on your Enterprise		
	Best Case	Worst Case	Highest Probability Case
①	Enterprise Strategic / Tactical Response	Enterprise Strategic / Tactical Response ②	Enterprise Strategic / Tactical Response
		③	
①	Enterprise Strategic / Tactical Response	Enterprise Strategic / Tactical Response ②	Enterprise Strategic / Tactical Response
		③	
①	Enterprise Strategic / Tactical Response	Enterprise Strategic / Tactical Response ②	Enterprise Strategic / Tactical Response
		③	
①	Enterprise Strategic / Tactical Response	Enterprise Strategic / Tactical Response ②	Enterprise Strategic / Tactical Response
		③	
	Enterprise Strategic / Tactical Response	Enterprise Strategic / Tactical Response	Enterprise Strategic / Tactical Response

The gap between the current enterprise "As Is", and the "picture of future success" that you have painted as you have analysed the competitive environment and your own enterprise, represents a "strategic gap" that will require thoughtful actions to close.

Strategic Themes

Defining three or four high-level strategic themes, that break the strategic gap into actionable focus areas, can provide a logical basis for setting goals and objectives. These then lead to complementary initiatives that move the enterprise in the agreed strategic direction, rather than to "organisation death through 100 uncoordinated initiatives". Some consider strategic themes as an Enterprise's "pillars of excellence". In one of the enterprises I served, the strategic themes were operational excellence, strategic partnering, excellent client service and a compelling place to work. Each strategic theme should have one strategic result - a more manageable basis for developing the enterprise than the very detailed strategic plans that I have seen in some enterprises.

It can be helpful to develop this thinking into a "strategy story" that can be the centre of a drive to communicate the strategy throughout the enterprise. One approach to injecting real richness into the story is to have subject matter experts for each theme. They then use their expertise to break each theme into a set of strategic objectives - charted to your point of view on how the enterprise will create value for your customers and other stakeholders. This can be illustrated in a "strategy map", that can be used to both validate the coherence of your objectivesm and aid subsequent communication. The following example is for an information systems consulting enterprise that identified operational excellence, building [growing] the business and understanding stakeholders (inc. customers) as three strategic themes during a strategy day. Note that the diagram includes objectives (with arrows to illustrate cause and effect), prioritisation of some of the objectives and a segmentation in four dimensions (Financial, Stakeholders, Business Processes and Employees & Infrastructure), that the Enterprise planned to use in a Balanced Scorecard to assess performance each month.

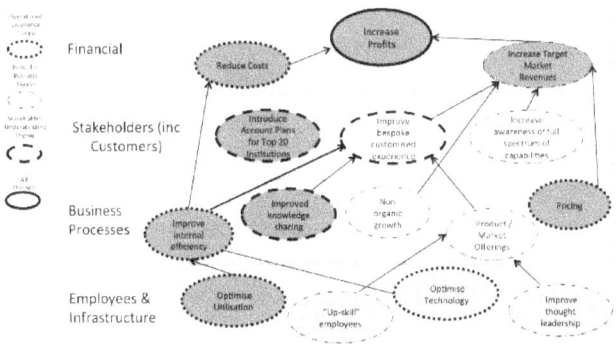

In my experience, a key to achieving value from investing effort to develop such themes, is to ensure that the initiatives involved are consistent with both the stated values of the organisation and the stated Enterprise strategy. This necessitates employees understanding the Enterprise's values AND sensing the linkage between the initiatives they are investing their time in and the stated Enterprise values. Engaging environments inspire discretionary effort - to achieve and maintain such engagement, Leaders need to demonstrate values that resonate with the spectrum of enterprise stakeholders (as opposed perhaps to only some of the employees' wallets). Personally, I have been fortunate to see the benefits that flow from the culture that emerges - not least during my time on 16 Squadron in the Royal Air Force and at Andersen Consulting / Accenture. Both organisations were less reliant on checks to ensure process compliance and more importantly, were able to maintain strategic direction through "fogs" of intense competitive rivalry.

Harnessing "Big Data" and Business Intelligence / Analytics

"80% of the World's data has been created in the last 24 months"

Rich Clayton Vice President Analytics, Oracle

"Every two days now we create as much information as we did from the dawn of civilization up until 2003"

Eric Schmidt, Google

The growing volume of business data[20] and the increasing numbers of devices directly connected to the Internet, is creating a huge opportunity to understand both our competitive markets and our own enterprises better. Some observers such as Paul O'Riordan, Oracle's Head of Business Analytics for the UK and Ireland, argue that we are now at a tipping point as a result of:
- the widespread availability of tablet computers (that provide a more engaging user experience),
- the Power of technology both hardware (that is allowing database utilities to be embedded onto chips), and business analytics software that is easy to use by business line managers (as opposed to IT specialists),
- the ready availability of data - including unstructured data.

---

[20] Including social media, all the transactions we undertake on the Internet, the sites we visit on the Internet, our locations as we use our Smartphones

With such a mass of data and analytical tools, an increasing challenge is to ask the right questions in order to extract actionable information and knowledge. The tools I have mentioned earlier in this chapter provide a foundation for developing questions that will help surface actionable insights.

For example a mobile telephone company's 5-Force analysis may have identified the likelihood of increasing competition as a result of a new entrant to the market. On the basis of your experience, you believe that it is easier to retain a customer than to attract a new customer, so you decide to seek to understand more about the customers that have cancelled their contracts over the last six months. You commission analysis to establish whether there are any "patterns" amongst the customers that have left. This analysis highlights a significant number of customers who use an average of between 600 and 750 MB of data a month are leaving. These customers are only light users of calls and texts. Analysis of your competitors offerings, show that one has a monthly plan that includes 750 MB of data but much lower call and text allowances at a cost of only 60% of your charges. Armed with this analysis, you decide to offer an additional option that includes 750 MB of data but less calls and texts. As the "targets" appear to use email more than texts or voice calls, you also decide to email these customers when they reach the 11-month point of their 12-month contracts. When you go to thank the person who did the analysis for you, she demonstrates that the Business Analytics software tool is really easy to use - with lots of "drag and drop" options and no requirement to write code. You decide that the tool should be built into a tablet application, with appropriate security controls to safeguard corporate data, and then distributed to all members of your Leadership Team.

The same Data Analytics tools can be used to help match individuals skills, capabilities, availability and aspirations to vacant roles, tasks and initiatives – provided of course that the necessary data is captured! Where such a people data bank is established, it can provide information to help leaders make better decisions. The visible data can help nudge people in the right direction. Furthermore it can provide them with the confidence to move away from the sort of 20th Century centralized command and control approaches that constrains agile performance. Holding relevant people data can then speed planning, speed business decisions, and help leaders identify problem areas earlier and make improvements faster.

Institutionalizing the capacity to change

> "Organisations need people who can meet the dual demands of discipline and stretch."
>
> Ghoshal and Barlett 1994[21]

Before discussing implementation of actions, four comments about change processes.

1. Organisations that approach change initiatives with a "Learning Mindset" are much more likely to institutionalise the capacity to change effectively into their DNA.
2. Change is unsettling and individuals need support and time to learn and implement new ways of working – some decline in enterprise performance should be planned to avoid unfortunate surprises / unplanned budget / performance variances.
3. Visible, on-going sponsorship of the change process and the new ways of working, by senior leaders helps people recognise that the new ways of working are real and not just "flavour of the week". Moreover, setting clear expectations that efficient optimisation of current performance, innovation and effective development / change management of new capabilities are necessary (Professor Jane McKenzie of Henley Business School refers to this as "Developing Ambidexterity: A Leadership Challenge to Engage Both Sides of the Organisational Brain"). The change processes themselves, when implemented effectively, help develop your next generation of leaders at all levels in the organisation.
4. Involving your high performers in the development of the new processes and systems, and perhaps as super users, represents a win-win for both the individual and the enterprise. During my time at Accenture we had an Action Learning programme for the next generation of Partners in one of the operating groups

---

[21] Ghoshal. Sumantra, Barlett, Christopher A. "Linking organizational context and managerial action: The dimensions of quality of management", 1994

that involved the identification and development of capabilities needed for the evolving marketplace.

Your "To Be"

"Plan for your future because that is where you are going to spend the rest of your life"

Mark Twain

Armed with your positioning of your enterprise on its S-Curves, an assessment of the competitive environment (from the Porter 5 Force and PESTEL analyses), your considerations of your organisational effectiveness (from your 7-S analysis), and your thinking about different scenarios for your enterprise in your competitive environment, you can make an informed judgement of future potential. A good start point is to consider, in revenue terms, three alternative "futures":

- Business as usual.
- Revenues that can be achieved if a full commitment is made to continuous improvement actions.
- Revenues, that you assess are achievable, if you evolve your strategic direction and are successful in building the capabilities needed to execute the change.

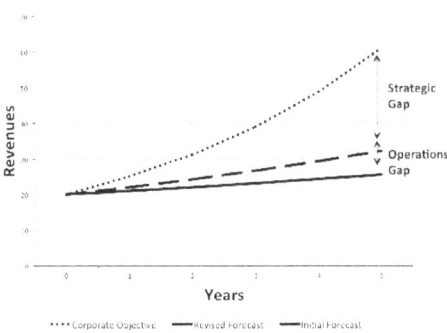

Setting strategic Direction

"There are risks and costs in a program of action, but they are far less than the long-range risks and costs of comfortable inaction"

John F. Kennedy

The strategic themes identified should help the setting of goals that will close the strategic gap shown on the chart above. For example, you may have concluded that you are not optimally pricing your products / services and this could form one of your goals. An objective to help achieve this goal could be a 3% improvement in the margin on new contracts. This could be supported by an initiative to develop a new pricing tool that would enable all relevant costs to be built into estimates more efficiently and consistently. Measures and targets could then be put in place to enable the management team to assess progress in achieving the goal on a monthly basis and then make any adjustments. This will only hold good if the measures are appropriate so please keep the following in the forefront of your mind (and do not delegate the development of measures to individuals who do not understand the content of the higher levels of the pyramid).

Measure the **Right thing in Right way** ═ **The Right Result**

Returning to the pyramid I introduced earlier, I encourage you to reflect on a business change you have introduced. Consider the extent to which there was a transparent and coherent rationale - that linked the targets and measures you used to assess business performance - through initiatives, objectives, goals and strategic themes to the visions, core values and mission at the top of the pyramid.

Initiative Planning

Too often during my business life I have heard arguments that enterprises would suffer death from 100 uncoordinated initiatives. Taking for a moment the position that "perception is reality" I see three sources for such perceptions:

a. Management had not explained how the initiatives would contribute to achieving the enterprise vision, OR
b. The initiatives were uncoordinated, OR
c. Unintended consequences emerged during the life of the initiatives.

I believe that the strategic theme approach outlined above, coupled with the pyramid breakdown to the level of measures and targets, should address points a, and b, so I am going to focus this section of the discussion on a technique to reduce the likelihood of unintended consequences from initiatives. I believe that the use of this technique, combined with the establishment of rigorous checkpoints to validate whether initiatives underway are still relevant, will reduce the probability of your colleagues suggesting "death by 100 or 1000 for that matter, uncoordinated initiatives"!

Jerome Glenn of the Antioch Graduate School of Education in New England created a "Futures Wheel" technique back in the 1970s to identify visually the potential consequences of trends and events. Over the years it has also been used successfully in decision making to choose between options and in change management to identify visually the consequences of change. The technique can be a useful complement to unstructured brainstorming as it helps organise thinking and provoke relevant questions rather than encourage a rush to a list comprising the first consequences people can think of.

To start a Futures wheel, a short statement of the change to evaluate, is positioned in the centre of a blank piece of paper. Then, events or consequences following directly from that development are positioned around it. Next, the (indirect) consequences of the direct consequences are positioned around the first level consequences. This process then continues for third and forth level consequences etc.

The following steps show how a Futures Wheel can be constructed:

1. Write the change that you need to consider in the centre of a flip chart or a blank sheet of paper - this could be for example an event, a trend, a problem, or a possible solution to a business issue.

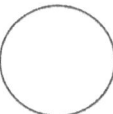

2. Brainstorm possible direct consequences of that change. Write each consequence in a circle, and connect it from the central idea with an arrow. For example, the direct consequences of imposing a 15% budget cut could be the cancellation of an IT enhancement project, no external training, a hiring freeze preventing recruitment of new staff and restrictions on travel expenditure - including perhaps Sales staff flying on low cost airlines rather than in Business class.

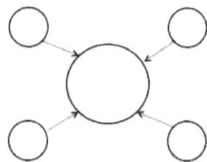

3. Brainstorm all the possible "second-order" consequences of each of the first-order (direct) consequences - for example the consequences of a hiring freeze maybe an inability to replace

retiring staff, a delay in the recruitment of a planned office a manager and no work for the recruitment manager

4. This process is then repeated until the potential consequences are exhausted.

A completed Futures Wheel for the 15% budget cut issue mentioned above is as follows:

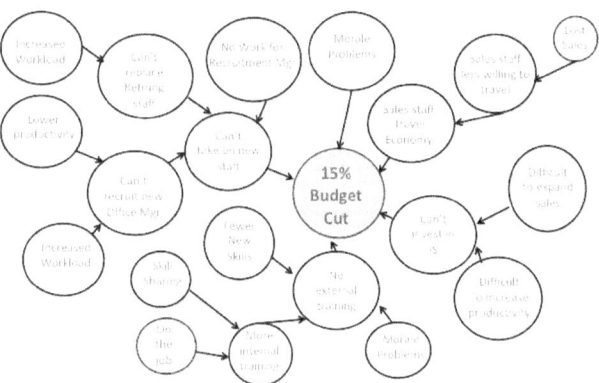

Please note how the interconnecting lines can make it easier to visualize interrelationships of the causes and resulting changes. By focusing attention on direct and indirect consequences, "Futures Wheels" can assist in developing ideas and options in a thoughtful way. Moreover, in the process they reduce the likelihood of unintended consequences surfacing as you develop the capabilities needed to execute your strategy.

Black Swans

Back in the 16th Century there was an assumption in London that all swans were white, because the data available indicated that all known swans had white feathers. Sometime later an explorer identified a swan with black feathers in Australia and assumptions about the colour of swans had to be changed! The "Black Swan" term became a metaphor for a perceived impossibility that is later disproven and was used by Nassim Taleb in his books "Fooled by Randomness: The Hidden Role of Chance in Life and in the Markets" [22] and "The Black Swan: The Impact of the Highly Improbable"[23]. Nassim Taleb assesses almost all major discoveries as "black swans" – including the development of the Personal Computer and the Internet.

However rigorous your assumptions, and however astute your analysis of your operating environment and your enterprise performance, black swan "surprise" events will occur that have a major effect in your competitive environment. In our relatively recent past even large companies like Microsoft were caught to an extent off guard by the advance of the Internet; however, in hindsight it could be argued that the data was available to indicate the Internet's significance. The significances in the context of this discussion are two fold:

1. We need to grow in our leaders the capacity to recognize "unknown unknowns " (to use Donald Rumsfeld's explanation from the days of the second Gulf War) i.e. events that lie outside the realm of regular expectations, because nothing in the past can convincingly point to the possibility of the event.
2. We need to build enterprises that are resilient and agile enough to exploit such events and search for new competitive advantages.

---

[22] Taleb, N.N, "Fooled by Randomness: The Hidden Role of Chance in Life and in the Markets", 2004.
[23] Taleb, N.N, "The Black Swan: The Impact of the Highly Improbable", 2007.

Adaptive Planning - Agility without Anarchy

In many organisations the planning, budgeting and monthly review processes can be nightmares involving masses of Excel spread sheets. Arguments over the accuracy of data caused by formula maintenance issues, version control problems as multiple people make modifications and the overall "brittle" nature of even the best designed spread sheets are frequent. In these circumstances the planning and budgeting process itself can become an enemy of agility. I have seen "heavily siloed" enterprises, where the finance department is adamant that plans and budgets must be "locked down" by a given date and then not "reopened" until the next year's planning round (or if one is lucky, a the end of the first quarter).

During my period as a Chief of Staff of a consultancy enterprise, I became convinced that enterprises cannot afford this barrier to effectiveness. I now consider investment in tools, processes and training that enable a 5 quarter rolling forecast approach to be institutionalised, and end of month financial reports to be generated efficiently, effectively, consistently and speedily an essential operating cost in our agile world. Whist I have been a great fan of spread sheets since the early days of Lotus 123 and Supercalc, I do not believe that they are fit for purpose for collaborative planning and budgeting in the second decade of the 21st century. A good selection of cost-effective specialist planning tools are now available for enterprises of all sizes. These allow that enable more robust management / update of assumptions, easier collaboration, better productivity and a focus on what one set of consistent numbers mean, rather than wasting executive energy arguing about the correctness or otherwise of various versions of the numbers. Armed with one of these software tools, early each month leaders can discuss the business with the benefit of solid numbers, focusing on reasons for the variances and actions to close them. At a minimum, quarterly, the enterprise leaders can reassess the competitive environment and adjust the planning assumptions that drive the budgets - agility without anarchy.

Conclusion

To maintain an appropriate focus during strategy activities it can be helpful to keep in mind "3 Ds of Strategy".

1. Discussion:
    - Your people's assessments and the opinions of your customers, suppliers and other stakeholders:
        - What do you think we are good at doing?
        - What can we do better?
        - Where do you see the industry in 3 years?
        - What are our competitors doing?
2. Decision
    - Focus on outcomes (desired goal and plan to reach it).
    - How is value going to be delivered as market evolves?
3. Development
    - Robust planning.
    - Proactive management of status – Time / Scope / Project Organisation / Team Cost.
    - Visible sponsorship and championing of initiatives.

Please activate the QR code below (or type http://wp.me/P3ep12-tl into your browser) to reach a web page containing a number of templates and useful links to further information.

4 BUILDING STAKEHOLDER COMMITMENT

"More companies understand that a broader spectrum of internal and external stakeholders has a direct impact on their core business. Those that have engendered deep levels of engagement – what I call high relationship engagement – are far more successful in shaping that impact to their advantage."

Nadine B Hack – Executive in Residence IMD 2011

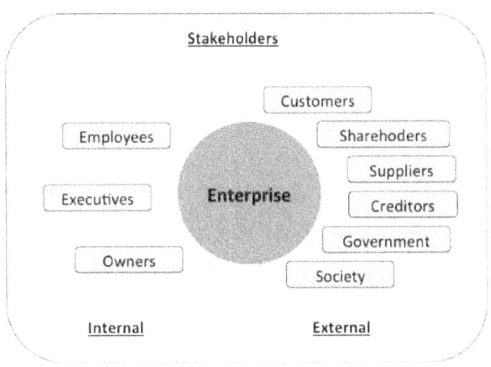

The premises for this chapter are:

1. Our competitive world is less certain, has mounting performance pressure, and in many cases a need to deliver excellent customer experiences with less loyal workers.

2. Engaging all stakeholders improve the enterprise's capability to sense changes in the competitive environment and spot opportunities and new sources of competitive advantage.
3. Both continuous improvement to existing products and services (the focus of Chapter 2) and improving enterprise agility to capitalize on changes in the competitive market (the focus of chapter 3) are more successful when individuals proactively engage – securing this discretionary behaviour can be a key to success.

Beyond Shareholder Value

"ANY organisation—a company, a government ministry, a charity, the local golf club—tends to become inward-looking if there is too little external discipline. Reams of academic literature have been produced to show how civil servants, however good-hearted, naturally act in their own interests, boosting their budgets, protecting their power, resisting outside scrutiny. So it is in private companies, except that managers there face discipline from competition with other firms, from the need to satisfy customers and from the demands of shareholders. Competition and pressure from customers have both become a lot more intense in most industries in the past two decades, all over the world, with beneficial effects on productivity and innovation."

The Economist

In Chapter 2, I discussed the Managing the Expectations of your clients and pointed out that I have used the same approach to managing the expectations of my own bosses over the years. I believe that there is value in extending the approach to all stakeholders of significance as a foundation for taking proactive actions to engage with each of the groups. Using the matrix below should help.

#	Stakeholder	Expectation	Alternative Expectation think about alternatives that would support a win/win)	Action

The dialogue involved in this process can provide a rich stream of insights that can help both current performance and your agility - by sensing changes in the competitive environment and amongst your value chain more quickly. I encourage all Leaders to develop a simple annual plan of activities to secure and then optimise these dialogues so that Stakeholder Engagement improves year on year.

Traction for the activities I have discussed in this book will necessitate securing "discretionary effort" from people. Much is being written about employee engagement and some researchers, such as John Hagel,[24] have argued that leading enterprises now need not just engaged people but people who have a real passion for their work and for creating value for customers.

> "While much work has been done to understand and improve employee engagement, employee engagement is no longer enough. Times have changed. Worker passion – defined by three attributes [Commitment to Domain and Questing and Connecting dispositions] rather than static skills that rapidly diminish over time – will be critical as we shift from a twentieth century world characterised by scalable efficiency to a twenty-first-century world amplified by scalable learning."
>
> John Hagel III

The "commitment to domain" refers to having an increasing impact - on a particular industry or component(s) of enterprise.
Individuals with the "questing" attribute, actively seek out challenges to improve their capabilities. Another way of looking at this has been

[24] *"Unlocking the passion of the Explorer"* John Hagel III, Deloitte University Press 17 Sep 2013.

articulated by Sir Clive Woodward[25], who emphasises the importance of individuals having a thirst for knowledge and learning – a real passion for their subject.

Those with the "connecting" disposition develop deep interactions with colleagues and the wider world and create trusting relationships that enable them to surface new insights.

In thinking further about the engagement / passion challenge, I think it is important to recognise that the objective is to raise the level of contribution of all the people in your enterprise - not just the senior people or the top performers. Two examples I like to quote to illustrate individuals in junior jobs having a sense of purpose, are a person on the Kevlar production line who when asked by Ellen Kullman, the CEO of DuPont what they were doing answered "Saving lives", and the man sweeping the floor at NASA, who told the then President that his job was "putting a man on he moon". To achieve such a strongly engrained sense of purpose we need to coherently explain how individuals activities contribute to achieving the vision for the Enterprise - this need something much more meaningful to an individual than the traditional mission statement.

The challenge then is to secure optimum business performance - now and in the future. To achieve this necessitates agile performance that grows customers that are more than satisfied as their needs evolve. A key to this in my experience is having people that are truly engaged and passionate about being better than their counterparts in other enterprises (now and in the future).

---

[25] The Rugby World Cup winning England coach.

Employee Passion

"Our world has changed and is changing in ways that call for a transformational response from organisations in attitudes and in ways of doing things, especially in ways of leading, managing and organising people"

Janice Caplan, 2013

Promoting a focus on the future, as well as today, is a foundation for developing the passion that will drive the discretionary behaviour agile enterprises need. Leaders at all levels in the enterprise who communicate a clear vision, a strategic direction that individuals can relate to and consistently (and visibly) live the enterprise values, create an environment that is much more conducive to having engaged people. In her 2013 Book[26], Janice Caplan argues that the key drivers of employee engagement are:

- The involvement and empowerment of people (with them effective support),
- An open, honest and supportive dialogue. This includes two-way, frequent communication with active listening and explanation of the bad news as well as the good.

How to build engagement?

Effective implementation of the ideas outlined in this book necessitates the involvement of people – moreover, empowered people that willingly commit discretionary effort to deliver a much higher level of contribution to continuous improvement, raising agility and improving stakeholder engagement.

"Managers and Leaders create the climate for engagement. They have to act in a way that inspire people to think for themselves and do 'whatever it takes' to fulfil the organisational purpose."

Professor Jane McKenzie 2014

---

[26] Caplan, J, Strategic Talent Development, 2013

Firstly, a quick win ...... walk about and talk to your people, show interest in them and thank them for particular contributions they are making. Quoting Tom Peters "there is no greater gift to the person or persons whom you are engaged than a heartfelt (as well as headfelt) acknowledgement of their contribution and fundamental human worth".

Secondly, recognise diversity – Different People have different circumstances, needs & motivators. Actions that are "tuned" to individuals will therefore be the most effective in raising commitment and employee engagement. We should expect that for some people, your enterprise will be the most important thing in their life – for others it will but one of a portfolio of interests. I believe that it is helpful to think about your people in a number of different "dimensions" as you consider potential actions to improve commitment and engagement. As an aid to better understanding your people you may like to consider where you assess they are on the following five dimensions:

1. Length of Service

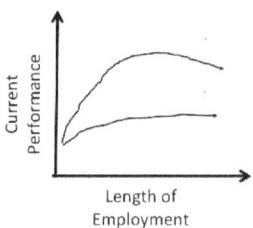

As a gymnastics coach in my youth, a frequent challenge was to help performers rise above "performance plateaus". This involved a mix of raising their technical skills and giving them the confidence to raise their performance to the next level. For example adjusting a gymnasts technique so that they achieved more height in a backwards somersault, as a prelude to introducing a twist into the somersault (which would generate the performer more points for difficulty and risk). This was achieved most consistently by taking the performer through a sequence of development steps to give them more time in the air and the confidence to "go for it". A skill was identifying those with the potential to rise above the current performance level and then form a programme of actions to exploit the potential. Applying this to the talent in your enterprise – who do you have that is operating at a plateau but has the potential to contribute more? Should you consider them for a move to a new role, for a training course to raise their skills, or can you involve them in a special project for example?

2. Personal Ambition

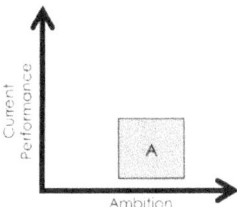

Taking this thinking a stage further, consider the level of ambition that each employee displays. Then ask whether the individual's level of ambition is realistic, and if so whether it is being adequately "fuelled" by you and your colleagues. Do you have any individuals in segment A (above) that have particular development needs that would need to be addressed before they can raise their current level of performance? Do they need proactive coaching to better align their ambition and performance?

3. Future Potential

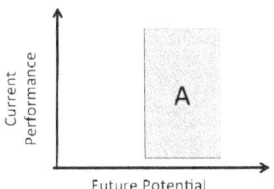

How much potential does each of your people have? It can be helpful to think of future potential as a combination of ambition and a personal engine to propel the individual along the journey towards the ambition's destination. Is there a mismatch between current performance and future potential? If there is, how can you help the individual to close the gap? Are the people in Segment A gaining sufficient personal satisfaction to be fully committed to your enterprise?

4. Value to the Enterprise

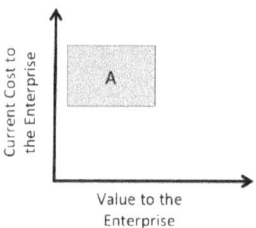

Plot a cross section of your people onto this graph. Do you have people in Quadrant A that need a performance improvement plan?

5. Individual Satisfaction

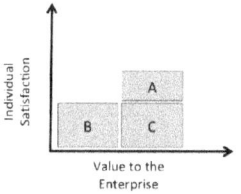

Do you have people who are contributing great value to your organisation that are not gaining individual satisfaction from their work? Those who are in the area shown as Box A in the graph are at particular risk of moving to new employment since they "feel" the benefit of some satisfaction. You might like to consider special projects or other responsibilities for people in this category to raise their level of satisfaction. It would also be prudent to consider succession plans in particular for people in this group and those in category C. Finally, consider what impact people in category B are having on the rest of your employees and seriously consider whether they have a future in your enterprise.

A meaningful dialogue with each of the people you are directly responsible for can flow from:

- The insights on your people that you have gained,
- Your understanding of your enterprise strategy (and in particular the strategic themes driving your goals and objectives).

This dialogue should agree personal commitments to the enterprise and enterprise commitments to the individual and provide a launch pad for improved commitment and performance - moving people up the commitment ladder. In an ideal world this would form the basis of a personal development plan for the individual and also be recorded in an enterprise system that allows these interests to be visible when decisions are being made on appointments or the staffing of initiatives. Approaches such as this can facilitate proactive management of the talent you have in the organization so that you achieve the win-win-win of better achievement of enterprise goals, more satisfied people and better development of the capabilities needed for future success.

> *"Great leadership is about creating a free and open conversation within a framework of shared values, share visions and shared understanding."*
>
> *Janice Caplan*

The Times 100 Business Case Studies[27] includes an example of the approach to talent management used at Siemens that achieves these ends. People are developed and matched to the tasks needed to realise the Siemens vision. The Siemens' talent management philosophy involves making sure that every employee is provided with the guidance and support to achieve their full potential (not just the high flyers).

---

[27] The Times 100 Business Case Studies, "Creating a high performance culture - A Siemens case study" http://businesscasestudies.co.uk/siemens/creating-a-high-performance-culture/talent-management.html#axzz2tlteOnzc

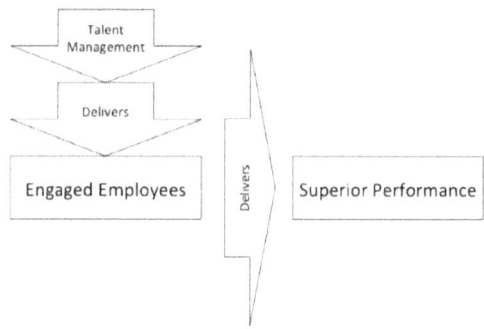

The outcome of the process is transparency between the enterprise strategy and the talent development plans for each individual. Targets relevant to the role and responsibilities are cascaded to each individual. Through meeting these personal targets, each individual optimises their contribution to the achievement of overall enterprise targets. Individuals are consequently clear about the impact of their performance and the consequences for their own development. The information collected during this process (generally "owned" and updated by the individual concerned), is recorded in an enterprise system, so that when roles need to be filled the enterprise system can be queried to produce a list of people that have the potential and interest for the role.

Future Shape of the Winner

The Tom Peters "Future Shape of the Winner"™ takes the 7-S thinking described in Chapter 3, a stage further by using a Gyroscope as a metaphor that embeds the essential requirement of maintaining alignment as the overall enterprise moves (potentially at high speed in our agile world).

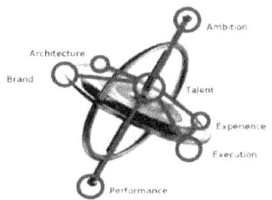

Tom Peters Company "Future Shape of the Winner ™"

It recognizes that a combination of dynamic forces in an enterprise interact constantly to find a natural balance as the enterprise strives to achieve its desired outcomes. For example:

- The experience that customers feel as the talent in the enterprise brings the brand to life.
- The architecture the enterprise evolves to support the execution of the services and products your customers experience.

Inherent in the approach is a balance of "systems plus passion" - a foundation of the Tom Peter's client work over 30 years. It considers excellence in 3 axis:

Performance	Experience	Execution
How well are the enterprise's people performing in relation to achieving the enterprise's ambition?	What do your customers experience when in dialogue with your enterprise?	How can leaders enable their talent to deliver the highest quality work output that they can?

Linked to the Future Shape of the Winner ™ is an internet based "Excellence Audit" ™ - a 360-degree assessment instrument that has been developed to capture the thinking of the key workers in an enterprise from the perspective of both current performance and the future. It enables enterprises to assess how they shape up against a

"Template" of an Excellent Company and to focus development efforts in the most promising areas.

Enterprises in a spectrum of industries from manufacturing to financial services have used the audit to help form improvement agendas. The Enterprises involved have faced a variety of situations including relocation of manufacturing, new services businesses and enterprises that have concluded that they cannot cost cut their way to success. Use of the Audit has helped galvanize the leadership teams involved around a new agenda. Moreover, insights from an Excellence Audit ™ have helped Leadership Teams understand why some of their change programmes are running well, while others are a source of frustration.

This involvement of people in identifying the priorities for action is another example of how Leaders can practically enhance employee engagement / passion – as long as they act on the audit report! One approach to doing this is to form project teams led by individuals who are considered to have potential to be next generation leaders. They can address the highest priority capability gaps and develop actions (including securing top management sponsorship), to close the gaps between current performance and the levels identified in an Excellence Audit™ as necessary in future.

Please activate the QR code below (or type http://wp.me/P3ep12-tn into your browser) to reach a web page containing a number of templates and useful links to further information.

5 CONCLUSIONS

In conclusion, I encourage you to engage your people in identifying continuous improvement opportunities, changes in your competitive environment and the consequent changes that are merited in your enterprise's strategy, structure, systems, staff, skills, style and potentially shared values. Embedding this involvement, into your "enterprise DNA", will serve as a robust foundation for developing your enterprise capability for a more agile future. Moreover, I believe that this will provide a foundation for raising the engagement of your employees and through them your overall operational excellence and enterprise agility.

Finally, a quotation that I believe articulates most clearly a sense of ambition that addresses the themes in this book.

> *Excellence demands we define a path of continuous improvement, constantly challenging existing processes. It also requires us to embrace change so we are in the right place when new opportunities open up. Excellence also means attracting the best talent in the marketplace and giving them the skills and opportunities they need to become high-achievers. We are committed to living a high-performance culture.*

Siemens Website February 2014

HUW MORRIS

6 BIBLIOGRAPHY

Caplan, J, Strategic Talent Development, 2013

Chandler, Alfred D., "Strategy and Structure: Chapters in the History of the American Industrial Enterprise", 1962.

Downes, Larry & Nunes, Paul, Big Bang Disruption: Business Survival in the Age of Constant Innovation, 2014

Edelman Trust Barometer
http://www.edelman.com/insights/intellectual-property/trust-2013/

Ghoshal. Sumantra, Barlett, Christopher A. "Linking organizational context and managerial action: The dimensions of quality of management", 1994

Peters, Tom & Watermann, Robert, "In Search of Excellence", 1982

Peters. T, Phillips, J. Watermann. R, "Structure is not Organization", Business Horizons, June 1980

Pettigrew, Andrew M, "The Politics of organizational decision-making", 1973.

Taleb, N.N, "Fooled by Randomness: The Hidden Role of Chance in Life and in the Markets", 2004.

Taleb, N.N, "The Black Swan: The Impact of the Highly Improbable", 2007.

The Times 100 Business Case Studies, "Creating a high performance culture - A Siemens case study"
http://businesscasestudies.co.uk/siemens/creating-a-high-performance-culture/talent-management.html#axzz2tIteOnzc

Tushman & O'Reilly, "Ambidextrous organizations: Managing evolutionary and revolutionary change", 1996

World Economic Forum Outlook on the Global Agenda
http://www.weforum.org/reports/outlook-global-agenda-2014

ABOUT THE AUTHOR

After school in Hertfordshire (just North of London in England), Huw Morris spent 3 years at Physical Education College where a primary interest was coaching Gymnastics and organising International Competitions. He attended the International Olympic Academy in Olympia in 1976 and the World Student Games in Sofia in 1977.

From 1977 to 1993 he served as a Royal Air Force Officer in the United Kingdom, Germany and the United States. Initial appointments in Finance and Human Resources were followed by a number of generalist roles that included Aide de Camp for a Commander-in-Chief and the RAF New Management Strategy Team in the Ministry of Defence. While in the latter role he conducted research into culture change for a dissertation.

Huw graduated with an MBA from Henley Business School in 1993 and after a period of Business School teaching he joined Andersen Consulting in 1996. His appointments included Quality Management, Practice Strategy and Global Industry Programmes for Food & Consumer Goods, Chemicals and Utilities. Following Andersen Consulting becoming Accenture and a Public Company he served as Director of Operations for the Resources Industry Group and as Chief Technology Officer for Accenture's Swiss based Intellectual property company.

In 2007 Huw joined the then LECG – a NASDAQ listed Finance and Economics Consultancy. He served as European Chief of Staff until FTI Consulting acquired the European assets of the company in 2011. After a period as European Director of HR for FTI Consulting he founded Efficienarta to focus on Executive Development and Corporate Governance Consulting. Huw qualified as a Chartered Director in 2010.

Huw Morris is married with two boys – aged 22 and 18. His interests include skiing and mountain biking.

www.ingramcontent.com/pod-product-compliance
Lightning Source LLC
Chambersburg PA
CBHW071755170526
45167CB00003B/1042